MW01257398

A SHOT
IN THE DARK

Poems by
ERROL RUBENSTEIN

Potter's Wheel Publishing House
Minneapolis

A SHOT IN THE DARK by ERROL RUBENSTEIN

Published by POTTER'S WHEEL PUBLISHING HOUSE
MINNEAPOLIS
MN 55378

www.POTTERSWHEELPUBLISHING.com

© 2024 Errol Rubenstein

errol-rubenstein.com

Cover photo by David M. Wong

ISBN: 978-1-950399-21-5

LCCN: 2024933688

To my mother and father, with love and gratitude

A Shot in the Dark is a work of consciousness and conscience. Powerful poems of love, separation and eventual reunion chart a difficult journey toward a mature relationship that admits freely of "questions without answers." Arresting imagery threads through these poems, a "visible music" at home in the nighttime ambiance Rubenstein evokes, ravishing "with its gabled house of stars."

—Thomas R. Smith, author of *Medicine Year* and *Storm Island*

A Shot in the Dark is an atmospheric collection that wrestles with existential questions, turning over alienation, estrangement, and terror in order to uncover what is, ultimately, sufficient. Rubenstein's poems offer a keen awareness of time and how much of it remains, as well as an exploration of how it might be best spent. Through beautiful pockets of imagery and lyricism, these poems attest to the power of art and the fierce joy that holds humans together. *A Shot in the Dark* fights through mistakes, angst, and regret to hold the door open for redemption.

—Claire Wahmanholm, author of *Meltwater*

CONTENTS

IV

V

I

VISIBLE MIST

I listen to the absence of sound,
a roaring silence.
I seethe and boil.

There are mysteries to behold,
mysteries all around us,
a plethora of signs and portents.

Nature...God made manifest.
There is nothing that compares.
Man is insignificant, in the face of it.

I sing about the things I cannot explain:
    Sentient computers with legs,
        What happens after we die,
            The body asking questions of itself.

I fill my mind, my heart:
    The basic goodness in people,
        The impulse to altruism,
            The solidity yet transience of the world.

        The puzzle of being.

How is it that the water is emptied from the pitcher
yet the glass never overflows?

How we delude ourselves, yet are steadfast in our beliefs—
How illusions are useful, even when invisible and unaccounted for.

The miracle of birth. The ever-changing seasons.
The wheel that spins and the absences that define us.

One must have a capacity for wonder.
Look up at the stars and pray.

ARS POETICA

How do we begin?
We have questions.
We ask. I am worried
that I will get locked
in a cage of my own
making, a cage
made of bone and skull.

PERSEVERANCE

Sometimes I reach for things that should not be reached for—
an arrow shot from a bow, a cup of golden cherries,
things that are not mine for the taking,
undisguised, raw, unrefined as salt.

The scope of my life has narrowed drastically, a narrowing that sustains
me, that leads me to conversations that leap and hop like some confused
rabbit; conversations with friends and loved ones that are my meat

and marrow, the sustenance of my spirit that draws me to seek
out the company of a friend in need. On no brown parchment
is there written a clause that says I would lose
the battle but win the war—

it is my struggle to lead a good life, that pushes me to the fringe,
to a place where my sword and shield are laid at the feet of a bronze
Buddha, illumined by candles, left as an offering of peace. My tormented

spirit I must live with day in and
day out, I must endure.

The wave breaks neatly on the ocean's surface—
the break in me will need time to heal.

THE FAILURE OF THE STONES

I

In the failure of stones
A flash of dust,
In the journey of the flesh
A fire in the bones.

Remember the water
And the whisper of wind,
With the patience of the dead
Waits the river daughter.

Near the fangs of flowers
After the beasts of winter,
A light fills the vase
Where a silkworm cowers.

II

Have I the courage to curse the sun?
Near the silence of small waters
I crouch and tremble.

NOCTURNE

Night falls like a mask
Your lips, red rills
The hills remain
No thunder, no rain
Silence like a curtain.

Biting my tongue
Until it bleeds
Until I can no longer speak
Until I can barely breathe
I manage to survive with heart intact.

White absence—
The judge's wig on the bench
The shirt on the court
The chalk on the board
The fallen snow.

IMPRESSIONS OF THE NATURAL WORLD AS NIGHT FALLS

Remember how it goes: clouds, water, light, stars.

Clouds and an evening wind—
it cleaves the sides of buildings
and splits open doors like a serpent:

The clouds rise on a risky wind
as the sun sinks, lonely and low, burning,
descending as night, obsidian, lets fall its shawl.

Clouds may wish to die, the wind to whisper,
the air bleed, the water weep,
but I will remain steadfast and I will not perish.

The moon bows to the shores
of the lake, and all the small misfortunes endured
over the years are turned back, slowly.

Nothing left to say. An empty cup. A cracked mirror.
A door once open, now shut.
The circle closes. The sky grows dark.

A slow rain begins.
The darkness I own bleeds outwards
covering grass and cracked earth.

These are the implements of despair.
Night falls. The white circle of the moon rises.
I am growing old. There are so many stars.

II

LAUGHTER INTO TEARS

Listen...there are little creatures everywhere:

They are on the streets, in cars, in bars,
and they need love. I lift my eyes to peer
out from the darkness that is inside me;

the blackbirds, the sleeping Monarch butterflies,
the tiny white moths huddling in the pit of my stomach.

And I weep for all of us.

GENERATIONS

I

Anything goes these days—

Drunken sprees, sexual forays at the reservoir—
a memory swims up: Arizona, a desert dotted with Saguaro
cacti, bodies flying out over the water,
a branch struck by a bolt of lightning
at midnight in a thunderstorm.
Pelting rain wrecking the evening,
a rope knotted to a tree branch, dropping
ungracefully into the water, swimming
side by side in the chasm, then dry,
eating birthday cake.

II

Anything goes these days—

No limits, absent parents,
disaster coming over the hills,
in the dark. Music floats.

My kids are young; I, an older father.
Children are eggshells, their minds float in the breeze,
take flight, soar like cherubim, lift up
heavenward, higher, higher.

All is process, growth, blooming, becoming.

III

Anything goes these days—

Our world is teetering—climate change, a war in Ukraine,
North Korea testing nuclear weapons. Stopping to think,

I worry about the future, my children's future,
this world we leave them is fragile
held in balance, nearing the tipping point.
I worry so much. Immortality not mortality.

AFTER THE DEATH OF GEORGE FLOYD

I pick up the phone to hear the soft hum of silence,
go out, walk down dark, empty alleyways—

a car flipped over in the middle of the street, lying
on its roof, a crowd of gawkers, police cars, an ambulance.

I see the poor with their cardboard signs, hungry, destitute.
There has been unrest, riots, looting, police brutality

and people crying out for justice, crying in the streets—
they do not want to die and lie six feet under.

The energy of the crowd is massive as a
mountain, could power a city, move a nation.

What is coming over that distant hill?
Not the rising sun but a massing

storm that when it arrives, will shake
the foundations of our lives.

WINTER'S SLEEP

These are the desolate, dark weeks
when nature in its barrenness
equals the stupidity of man.
        —William Carlos Williams

The world awakens to stunning weather—
tearing wind, cold, drizzling rain—

winter approaches like some strange animal,

airplanes are feathers in the sky—
with the first light of daybreak a skein of geese

take flight, head South for warmer air,
soar over snowy dunes, frozen lake, wings spread

on churning currents. Squirrels scatter, gather
acorns, store food for long frigid months.

High up on thin branches above wide, white,
iced fields and frosty lawns, eagles alight, build

nests, hunt for fish, scavenge carrion, pick
around in trash piles, snatch rodents and small

mammals from their burrows. In a cave in the woods
a black bear and cubs, unaware, curled like commas, sleep

through the season's long cold months. Even bees know
secrets denied us: secrets of wind and flower, of pollen, stamen, pistil—

the human race, so supercilious in our hubris.

Stop. Take a look:

Junkies bathe in amphetamine bliss, crack
and smack course through tired veins, while

a glance into the street reveals gang warfare, noise
rises to a fever pitch, the city's cries break open the night—

dreams of silence persist through long insomniac evenings.
Shootings in offices, malls, convenience stores, movie theaters, schools—
corpses multiply.

Students and parents fear a peer on a rampage: flying bullets
in hallways and classrooms—
a safe space to learn now a lost dream.

A man shot in the face. In a collision, twenty
dead, eight children, their futures unlit candle wicks.

Politicians stand on stages, deliver speeches in defense
of misguided beliefs, lies, vast oceans of misinformation

mislead

the masses.

After all the singing, after the chaos and the screams, a serious quiet.

The vast unknown beckons humankind—
purged of earthly cravings eventually we will leave all this behind—

mind, body and spirit—an ascetic purity,
like the residue of distilled vinegar.

In middle age we force desire from memory,
the stuff of dreams, a fading flame.

This notion becomes clear as the facets of a diamond,
an emptiness where I wonder whether loss is serenity...

and then we pretend to be ourselves.

THE OTHER SIDE

October, and a cold breeze out of the North.

A war is going on on the other side of the globe;
a war of one man's wishes, wishes
that come from a mind teetering on the brink of

madness.

People are dying. Children are dying.

Leaves crunch beneath my black sneakered
feet as I walk slowly through the empty
courtyard, sparrows gathered in a corner, conversing

in tiny voices, and my wife loves me and I her,
but there is a space between us that only words
can bridge, and the words are scarce.

They flit in and out of my mind like quantum particles.

I am alone and I am tired and lonely,
and my work has not been done,
and I am falling, failing:

I am growing old.

I fear tomorrow like I fear the lengthening
shadow of my body as I tread lightly, away
from the setting sun heading for the dark.

On TV war continues, and I sit howling
like a caged wolf at the carnage and loss

of life. I await the sunrise towards which
my whole being leans.

JOURNEY

I

My night of broken dreams ends with the dawn.
I watch a small bird perched in a tree
waking slowly, dark-winged; watch him rise
and wake and sing to greet the sun.

I, too, rise, and peer out the window.
But it is not the shape of water, nor the shape of mist
on the river, but the shape of something within
that is troubling my thoughts and crumbling my hopes.

Woken in the midst of sleep
I was suddenly crushed in the night, broken and battered
by a force beyond my understanding, a force
that came from nowhere, unbidden, unwanted.

And even before sleep
had taken me I felt my name
flee, vanish, until I sat nameless
staring into the dark.

II

I set out to walk.
Palms sweat-covered, heart racing,
thoughts flying. I am whipped in the wind,
blown around corners

and calm has fled, nervous energy
flits electrical, jumping the gaps like a stag leaping.
Like an ant that knows only the response
of his nervous system,

only the rapid movement
of legs and skedaddled direction,
so, too, do I move.

I return to the underground
garage and unlock my bicycle where it is chained
to the rack. I pedal

down the empty street. The rain holds off
as white clouds that dot the expanse of blue
give way to gun-metal grey that covers
the remainder of the sky. As I ride, rain threatens.

But I head for where the sun
escapes the chasing, leaden clouds
laid like a blanket across the blue.

III

The hurt never seems to fail me,
no matter whose instructions I follow—
my own or someone else's—no matter whose cajoling
I avoid or disobey; no matter if I try
or do not try, the hurt never fails me.

To channel this wounding and form phrases,
this is our disaster, and our need.

A horror. A tempest in the shape of words.
It makes one revel in the dust.

And the unknown variable—
what some call chance or dumb luck—
astonishes me with its gift that enables
me to fulfill my goals, my wishes, in crafting my art,
in delving into the written word.

It throws me back, leaves me
breathless, stunned.

IV

Yet I need love to sustain me
when all else fails—
when the words run dry,
when my concentration allows me
only five minutes of reading,
when I look at a stack
of books and am disheartened.

Love and art, the art of words,
the power of the written word—
the bulwarks that I need when
dark days, arriving like gloomy
sentinels, enter my life.

This will do. The future, wide
as the blue unforgiving sky,
tempered by my canopy of doubt,
will suffice and sustain me
as my heart overflows its loving cup, and I
dispense words from its vessels of secrecy.

SLEEP. LOST. HEART.

I have fallen out of touch,
dropped off the radar, disappeared
from the page.

The world has begun to narrow
again, with love's tunnel vision,
the vanishing point at which all hearts intersect.

I feel free and read at night until sleep
calls from a distant echo of childhood,
and I am enthralled yet again by my lover.

I have heard it say that we die every night
and my heart is as steel forged in flame.

There is music all around. My body wishes to sing.

III

DESCENT

The surface: crystalline, aquamarine,
as my love and I dive deeper, deep cobalt blue,
the light dimming as we

approach the wreck, bubbles like musical notes,
a symphony of submerged air, rise.
The pressure of seawater like a coffin,

breathing more difficult,
a troubling susurration; deeper and deeper
we dive, spears of light fading.

Into the dark, the all-encompassing blackness,
blindly we drop, lower and lower.
We grasp for handholds, iron mast,

side planks starboard, pocked, rudder rotted,
sails now destroyed and gone, the rusted hull,
the bridge and forecastle in gloom.

Fish slide by, barely visible,
self-absorbed, ignored by mantas.
We circle the deck,

eels appear from hidden hollows,
timid, frightened of discovery and danger.
The wreck; behemoth, corpse, Goliath

beneath the waves,
rusted steel and moldering wood.
A hundred or more sailors.

And the apparition of a skeleton
slowly, silently, slides into my view
and I wonder,

with my balding and graying hair,
how much longer until my own bones
are buried?

I hope to be remembered, pressed leaves
on a blank canvas, to have touched
a life, or saved just one child

from the whipping winds of youthful turbulence;
left on my grave, a garland of lilies will keep company
my soul in the hereafter.

We sight the bottom-most hold. An hour has passed.
We have air enough to last us until we surface.

A WHISPER OF RAIN

The future rushes to meet me from the silence among
the grasses. A sea of stars illuminates the evening sky.

I remember where I left you, softly sleeping, immersed
in a dream. I hasten back towards your sleeping form—

as I return, you awake from the backyard of your imaginings,
we embrace, plunging to the stars, living again in each other's

arms, the new day
dawning,
a spectacle of light.

I remember those years ago, the waiting room, you were cow heavy and
floral,
belly-swelled, a beautiful, fluted nightgown falling over tender knees and
long, lean legs;

time, like an infantryman, has marched onwards to the steely beat of a
drum,
moving along sluggishly, like a baby's progress across a patchwork carpet,

but always motion, nothing the same—
the changing traffic lights at night, the screeches, squeals, sirens,

and sibilance of the rain.

The thunder booms and wails, thunder
and pelting rain

shattering the glassy
        calm of night.

The thunder cracks again,
lightning hits and splits a tree,
a forked branch—
brown bark severed from trunk.

A murder of crows overhead,
the wind sighs,
the grass sings,
the high metal gate swings.

In the yard behind the house
where in spring sap rose,
the house of our dreams where
we face all our fears.

Every house is a prison,
Every prison, a house.

The time for mourning is past.
The time for mourning has not yet arrived.

NIGHT SKY WITH IMPLICATIONS

The sun set long ago: light is gone now
from the window at the back of the house.

The moon shines upon the spaces
where light has gone out.

Today I missed no one.
Tomorrow I may mourn.
Your love, for the moment, is all I need.

Let's make a hole in the sky and disappear.
Behold the star. Behold the moon. A door is open.
A light is shining through it.

I am tired enough for anything.
There is stasis.

I can only see to the horizon, and not
beyond it. And yet, I am the horizon itself. I am that line
one cannot see beyond.

And I often feel that I am nothing
at all. And you are nothing at all. But I am
what you have given me: the blooming, the being,
the becoming.

We are no longer empty.

Now I have found you, words are
feathers on the wing, salt in the mine, water in the glass.

Between the coming and the going is the infinity of sky.

AN ELEMENTAL FICTION

Dark river. Blue twilight. Gray dawn. Deep image. Solid state.
Shattered mirror. Incline plane. Creased handkerchief. Tiny spectacles.

Glass ornament. Sling shot. Iron mast. Pin hole. Nail file.
Bed spring. Cotton gin. Beer bottle. Storm drain. Knife blade.

Time on an eagle's wing; bird's talons grasp a rolled-up
piece of parchment, it perches there and does not fly.

If I could reach down and tear this pain from my heart...
If I could say just how I feel...
If only I could make up to you the hurt I have caused...

I am afraid of silence, enthralled by the blue unappeasable sky.

WAITING FOR YOU

You Leave

You are gone from me. I sit counting the minutes
and laying out letters like smoke.

I want you to talk to me again
with syllables of love, with the music

of your voice, with the blue
of your eyes.

Where have you gone?
I do not know. Still, I believe that I will

end up in your arms, breathing lightly into the hollow
of your clavicle, there just below your shoulder.

I reach out, lay my hand on the curve
of your hip and it is like nothing else in this world.

Meditation

I hold on tightly to my soul, it can be taken;
I ponder the mystery of yours.

What have we become?
We are shadows of water.

As if on the tip of an arrowhead, I am a point
of fear awaiting you. There is a patch of darkness.

I have turned my passion into a mountain,
yet my words are trapped in cages.

Moments of Doubt

I find neither love nor sorrow
as I sit and watch the hours pass.

The sky, filled with stars, a vast canopy of black,
pockets of light. Local time is nothing like time across the sea.

Events of the day shock, slap me into silence.
I am mute and hear nothing. I crouch

missing you and pining for lost time.

Dreams of Darkness Descend

I must have patience. I offer up prayers
hoping they are heard.

Sometimes I am certain that you will return to me.
More often I am simply finding my way, navigating these lonely hours.

But not here. Here I am lost.
Here there is only dry dust.

Without you I feel so alone, my shadow, my best
and only companion.

This darkness comes bleeding fire and is neither pure nor whole.

Psalms arrive, by and by, at twilight.

HURT

Our life, in which I have offended,
lies before me—
shattered glass.

I have whispered secrets to strangers,
committed transgressions.
Like blood that

astonishes, inflicted hurt.

So, I have damaged you; you are a broken ear of corn.

Moments, minutes, hours, days, months have passed
and I cannot put my foot back into
that river that brought us here.

You give me things to do,
I do them. This helps, you say.

So, we live parallel lives,
and I will try to be happy under your color.

Would you hold my hand while I told
you lies?
Would you stand with me if I showed you
my naked fear?

And yet there is hope, for tonight
signing off with you on the phone,
I said I love you; and, like a star newly born,
like the sun lighting a new
day, you said
the same.

This is the arrow hitting
the center of the target.

A LIVING DARKNESS

Tears fall as a dark star passes above—
I have driven this life's road in madness and much confusion.

I sense something coming over the horizon,
soaring, something prehistoric.

I look through a prism, make out the edges,
the corners, a ghostly shape.

I struggle silently with an obsession
with death. I find neither love nor sorrow,

I am alone, away from my family,
I am empty and broken.

Yet as I watch the hours pass, slip through,
I see you, my love, in your separate abode, and I miss you.

My mind, a thorny thicket in a garden
of my own making.

Hurting you with betrayals, with neglect, with care-
lessness, was a sin, a regret that I may never get over—

yet in the face of love, the pain diminishes.
I have hidden the truth behind a wall of shame,

I have not taken ownership for my actions,
nor been the husband I wanted to be.

But now I tell you without hesitation I have gone
to hear music when I could have been working

for all of our benefit, and there is honesty
held in my heart and mind, a seed, a root,

a young sapling bending
in the wind, never breaking.

A LIFE ABOVE GROUND

I live in shadow. My life, a leaf falling. I sit and things
are quiet, while inside there is a fluttering of wings, a dark life birthing.

I learned too late what I miss: home, cocooned family-life, gentle quotidian
gestures of love without regrets, you in my arms. Alone in this one-bedroom

cell loneliness and anger set aflame my soul, mind, hands.
This life spills out like water sloshing. I ask the open sky:

why does memory fail me—photographs of grandparents lost in transit.
I hesitate and am lost; must continue to mend fences

with you, my beloved. I have nothing of value left, only
confusion and doubt, mistakes and failings. Like a feather

in churning waters, drifting farther and farther away from all
that anchors me, I have embarked on a journey back to when

we were happy and discovering each other for the first time, two hearts
in tandem. I look through scrapbooked pages: first dates, the beginning of
our journey,

like tasting fresh strawberries for the first time. I see us with arms around
each other saturated with love. Time and determination will not allow me to

cease, but only to persevere even as we drift apart like schooners in a gale,
headed for different shores. My arms stretch out to you, yearning for your
touch.

Though love is all, why am I filled with dread?

WINDS

Night dented, I grab a fistful of patience. I tear
down walls between myself and others to get to the actual,
I wear a grey sackcloth, fringe the color of ashes.

The past is gone, irretrievable.

The hours fall away like boulders to a shoreline, and again, I mistake
fear for love. In days past I danced with angels, head held
high, bathed in light like some new cherub or seraph, but no longer...

yet still I find peace in the night; though lonely and alone
there is music to keep me company. I revel in the darkness, the silence
between songs, thoughts running through me like a parade of toy

soldiers. I wish those bright days would come again,
when I could see clearly and the murk did not obscure
my gaze, when the haze cleared, was lifted, when the sky had not

fallen away, when the gales of change were not
howling, ripping through me and transmuting
me into some new mad, monster,

some being who I do not know nor wish to be.

I have become alien to myself, my self-knowledge
now a thing of the past, something I have lost
trying and failing over and over to hold onto my belief in myself,

my confidence.

Only in that one place of sanity—
that small two-bedroom
apartment where my family lives—

only there is calm,
only there can I rest my mind,
only there do I cease seeking, looking for answers where there aren't any,
only there do I realize the questions are all wrong.

It is in my children faces, in their laughter, in the arms of my wife
around my neck, that I find any sort of rest, of peace. And friends
who bear me up in troubled times, whose words reassure

me when all seems lost, words that fall on my ears
at times with the force of a falling tree. I have detoured, detonated,

am at an alternate destination,
have left the sure and steady path

the comfort I lived some years ago when we took meals together,
when the soft lullabies put my young boys to bed—
I am headed down this new road I fear to approach, this road

winding through underbrush and thickets, thorns that rip and tear
my clothes, my flesh, as I live my days of work and struggle.

Claps of thunder thrum through me.
How many times must I change direction in order to get back home?

LOVESWEPT

Leaves on a swift, dark wind. I crave you, my beloved, I want
to know where we stand. No one-sided, executive decisions made--

only in harmony, the conflation of you and I. Like a wave
crashing over our prow, so does our compact shatter when I fail
you with lies, unjust accusations, slurs on your character—

I let you down and panic ensues, like the rush of water
over cliffs, fear that our burgeoning life together will not last.

A clear sight of the landscape, delineated points on our life's map.
I see the lack of food in the refrigerator, the mess in the living room,
books strewn across the floor, and you, overtired, overwhelmed, struggling

each day. I complain and accuse; a dearth of compliments, a want
of validation, a lack of tender touch. I strive for the in-between, the grey

area between extremes, my journey back to you,
the place where you smile and laugh.

How do you heal a wounded heart? Repeated apologies, promises
to improve. Does it bring healing? I am balanced on stilts, teetering.

I struggle to keep you content, takes all I have to give.
We persevere, battle through the changes—
new job, new house, new school for the children. Mistakes

made, but time repairs the hurt like grass and flowers awakening
in spring after a long, cold winter. My love for you
does not wilt; like a burning sun it shines on you and melts

the frozen places in your heart, heals the broken places.
At the edge of a lake, on the horizon, the sun rises.

We live again.

PASSAGES

Shadows

A bridge I cannot pass,
a gap I cannot bridge.

A page, torn and tattered.
Holes.

Children

On the pavement, where you, little lion cub,
and you, little screech owl, walk, grasping my index
fingers one in each, your tiny steps
making me wonder at the wonder of you.

The darlings of my eye.
Wolves' ears, two pairs.

Mysteries

Why do things happen the way they do?
Is there such a thing as fate? And several times
a day, there is no stopping the tears, yet I am slowly
learning how to be happy.

My belief—
It could not have been otherwise.

TWINNING

Much of the time I am moving about in darkness.

We try to set limits, instruct our twin boys on proper behavior,
but they are forces of nature, energy that stops
for nothing; chairs overturned, walls written on,
books thrown, controlled chaos that frightens me beyond words.

Yet there are also times of abundant joy:
we cuddle on the sofa, I read them stories.
They tell me the names of dinosaurs—
Iguanodon, Archeopteryx, Utahraptor.

One builds a structure out of blocks, with room for cars,
as a wave of anxiety overcomes me, breaks like thunder,
and I am completely overwhelmed, but I have the stamina to take care of
my children:

All I really need is love and patience. And work.

There are times when thoughts fly like birds out of my skull,
but I prefer raw experience—and this is the experience
of raising my twins, and it is like holding

a knife blade between my teeth.

PTERODACTYLS

A Fitness Room. Shadows on the walls
are Pterodactyls in flight. Exercise bands
on a rack, blank television reflects
pumping arms pacing the treadmill.

Then dinner, oatmeal and berries,
blue and bumpy. For a few hours
time stretches out like a taut muscle.

Blue balconies stacked like cards.

A rectangle of trees at the edge of my vision,
a commotion of birds twittering in turn, wheel
off to perch like sentries on broken branches.

The clock ticks away last light of a tired
day, sunset fades to unappeasable black.

Sleep, a distant fugitive, recedes further.

Visible music. In the night sky, out there in the beyond,
in the reaches of space, galaxies, translucent nebulae
of blue pillars, stars floating.

I am water. Waves move inside,
dance towards shore, one follows
another like obedient children.

My mind, rent. A tear, a flash, a spark.
I feel my son, such a small boy, curled up inside me.

In bed, staring blankly at the ceiling,
I see patterns the shapes of the dinosaurs
my son loves, the animals he adores,
the Pterodactyls that soar through his skies.

DAY'S END

The sun also ariseth, and the sun goeth down...
      —Ecclesiastes

Liquid night breaks and fades, sky turns pale
blue then gradually deeper, deeper, until
the clouds, the sunlight, the conversation of tiny
drops, clear as crystal, dance.

Rain falls, until, as we walk to school,
hand in hand, we take care not to slip
and slide on the pavement. I step forth,
leaving you in good hands,

and returning to my apartment, filled
with light and air, I think only of prayer—
music is all around me.

As an envelope holds a letter,
as a schoolbook has a cover,
as a ruler, numbers.

Later, I pick you up, your job done for the day.
You have played, sung, run, jumped, created,
destroyed, built, smashed—

been taught and taught in turn.

The sun sets, shines in its own blue twilight.

Often, I am waiting for the other shoe to drop.
Often, I wrestle with mortality.
Often, I wonder at you—

so perfect, here on this imperfect Earth.

Day's end and night falls like a caul.

Our spirits weary, we sleep,
our heads in halos of hair.

HOLY BOOK

I am brittle, skin cracking, flakes between my fingers.
I ride a slope of air heavenwards—such joy at times
that my tears speak, wash away rivulets of pain—
proof positive of elation, fervent emotion.

I pick up a Bible, my life written in those delicate leaves, and tear
names and events from its pages. I steal from this holy book—
thoughts of our matriarchs and patriarchs, their connection
to God, that God who I seek in troubled times.

Like a windstorm desecrating these holy words, I shudder
at this theft, but take comfort in Agnosticism,
for until I am struck down for these actions, I remain a skeptic.

Yet I take pause, for the sublimity of the natural world, the enormity
of our universe, beggars a reason, and if we must call it God,
call it God. Still, I conceive of a force, a force for Good.
But then is it just semantics? Splitting hairs? Maybe

my twin boys are proof enough,
for their perfection also beggars explanation.

In my mind there is white Pegasus,
gift to my children, on whose back they ride up, up to the sky,
amongst pillars of stars, to the very edge of the void.

BODY CHECK

Out of the mess that those who have tried to help
have made of me, I reclaim, I retain only
my bare skeleton, my broken heart, my battered brain.

And I have nothing in particular to do
so I unlatch my feet from my ankles

and set them next to my dirty sneakers in the hallway.
I peel back my ribs, one by one,

And lay them neatly in rows on the floor.
My legs, I lean in the corner like wooden canes.

My heart, old warrior, remains
in my hollow chest. I recline on a bamboo chair

and pull a blanket up to my chin, as I ponder my next move.
I unhinge my arms from my shoulders

and lay them across my chest. My lungs
expand and contract like two brave, windblown sails.

OF POETRY AND PILLS

My obsession with mortality less
now that my doctor is sane.
The last one, a robotic intonation,

questions without clear answers,
rifled off like machine gun fire—
a monotonous bedside manner.

The new one, intelligent, caring, easy
to talk to, just in time. Again.

Old medications stopped by my new doctor,
resulting in clarity, happiness, forgetful sleep,
untroubled dreams, no more insane laughter
in an empty room, no more associative leaps
disturbing my thoughts, no longer the angst, the stress, the...

so, we go on in this way, simplifying,
pruning, the mess that my previous
doctor made of the space in my head,
the doors I open and shut
both in love and rage.

And we will continue to prune and cut and reduce,
and there will be clarity, sanity, and yet

still there will be poetry.

And I fear that poetic life. So many poets:
Pound spending twelve years locked up
at Saint Elizabeth's, Wright struggling with mental illness,
Lowell with his manic depression,
only partially controlled by Lithium.
The suicides: Plath, Sexton and others—

I fear the dark, the irrational,
that in-between place, that wellspring
where poetry is shaped.
Womb where poems grow.

There is a line I will not cross between sanity
and madness: one slip and ahead of me
is delusion, hysteria, pure chaos.

Creativity and insanity are blood brothers,
and now I am deep into poetry,
and it is stronger than I can imagine.

I drain the glass, amber liquid down my throat.
Death. Light shines from the bottom up.

LESSONS

Last night, an hour of sleep. This morning—
difficulty reading difficult poetry. I reflect on things:
On the psych ward I learned that blunt edges are dangerous;
I learned from years of writing poems that there are words
among the silences, silences among the words. The trick
is to say it without saying it.

That reading and writing go hand in hand, like two schoolgirls.

This I have learned from my young twin boys:

Chop the whole thing down. Leave nothing standing. Use an axe.
Tear it up by the roots. Start over. Begin anew.

When you are young the space between people is greater,
they seem further apart. As you age the space narrows
and narrows until you surround yourself with yourself.

This I know:

The end is contained in the beginning.
At age 8 I knew my son was coming.
I waited 40 years, and he was born.

The thriving is what the striving is for, the living is what the giving is
for. Words come flying off the page, winged like bats.

I raise my arm and place stars in the heavens.
They shine in every blue twilight.

IN DARKNESS, IN LIGHT

Woe to him whose wilderness is within.
        —Friedrich Nietzsche

The heartbeat through the wall
The floor rising to meet me.
A dark hole through hell.
These are the roads of my song.
These are the colors of my days.

Kinnell said, "The wages of dying is love."
I say, "The wages of love is dying."

Now, movement, a reaching outward
into radiance, a dispersal of the dark.

Light entering water, breaking cloud cover,
silent patches of sky illumine what lies
earthward, tree roots pushing upwards.

This is my yard. Lilies and asters bloom, sky above,
hard earth below. I stand. The wind is strong,
sun gone, lights coming on; end of day

leaves us in peace. All over the lawn a certain feeling
happens, white waves of wind wash across the yard,
until the whole lawn is suffused with a dying light,

everywhere dirt resounds in music. Stopped
in my tracks, bones and tendons, flesh
and sinews lax, hanging loose, I seek

what I cannot find in the corners of the day:
a community of water and earth.

Here we rise up: My love and I wish to wake
from memory, holding on yet broken. Lightning
and thunder in the night as we lay in bed,

sheets pulled up to our chins, blankets in disarray,
our marriage, a tiny boat we are piloting.
Until our tears dry, until we no longer eat

the bread of sorrow, until we walk the path
of light and love, there will be no calling, no new life.

Where have you gone, yesterday's joy?
What does not belong should be burned.

The trees hide all beneath a canopy of green.
No more than what is given, no less
than what is asked for. We drift
through our days, seek
the echo that is love.

FIRE

I remember a beach, extensive, unbounded, water
laying down shells, wet sand
toe-dug and hand-sculpted. A sandbar, a floating raft
rearing its level planked surface above the water line.

Further out, sails passing left to right even before a sun
preparing to seep below the line of water and sky.
Nightly, the blaze of a bonfire lit a circle
peripheral; within, the orange and red glow, a dying sun.

Not thinking of future times, nor of past miseries—
for they were few—but reveling only in the present,
living it with everything: noticing, remembering,
never in fear or sadness, our hopes the center
of the heat of fire.

A moment etched in memory, yet how we have mellowed since!
In exchange for wisdom, comfort and calm, for maturity,

for a sober outlook, for a slowing down,
for a new respect of the simple life,

how we have come to accept what we have become.
How we have given up the flame.

MOON

We bathe ourselves in moonlight,
until we are soaked through, washed clean.

The light burns in us and is sacred.
The moon shines down and blesses our house.

It speaks to me, whispers words
to get me through the night,

to make life just that much more
bearable. The stars are holes in a cloak of black,

but starshine is a part of who we are.
There is silence, and a cold fire

within me flames to brightness with the flick
of a celestial switch.

We flash by, quickened into shadow
by the moments of our lives. Spring turns

to summer, turns to fall and we have not changed,
have now embraced our life.

The moon looks down on all of us
as we sleep;

and I feel,
that, where once we lived lives as distant

as the moon from Earth, life now seems
within reach, something

we have achieved, something that needs
only more patience and faith

to continue as the Moon spins
in its elliptical orbit.

I lean into our togetherness, learn
from the past

when there was sadness,
when things grew difficult

and we lived under two roofs on stages of silence and sorrow,
when I realized that to want is to fall.

Those days I moved through my own solitude
in search of us, in the moonlight—I failed, failed

and everything I touched turned to dust.

We are but moments, fireflies against black.
Hard lessons, then—

days when I would wake
filled with darkness, in the net of my own undoing

and know what was necessary
for us to continue: honesty,

patience, faith—the foundation
of the structure we have built,

like one of those houses
our twins build from blocks—the leaning

edifices with sharp angles,
and doors that open.

A LOVE SUPREME

My love and I change and grow, are transformed, transfigured
from responsibility to service. Clearer and clearer is our duty to others,
like sentries at the door of Altruism, that quality that makes us human.

Nothing more remains of the urge to idleness. Desire long held
in arrears appears again in the back of the psyche where, lying
in wait for the season to arrive, begins a slow journey homeward.

I suffer from unending desire and the graying of age.
We felt awkward on day one; now we are old pros.

Night will come with its gabled house of stars as we lift
packs in the wind, are blown from place to place, and the rain, in sheets
of sorrow, falls earthward drowning cracked soil and dust. Summer arrived

yesterday bringing cold light filtered through bare
branches, igniting the field, flaming the willow trees to brightness.

The shadow looms above. Blue darkness and green
envy stain the edges of my days. Referencing
the real leads to a solid grasp of beauty.

Heart lifted, world held in the palm of my hand,
fingers on the edges of my cup that runs over,
a yearning for days gone by, before pants hung loose on hips:

Before the breaking and breaking again.
Before more and more blood.
Before the teeth and the blood.

No temporary return. No holding on with hope for reprieve.
Footsie beneath the covers: an attempt at reconnection, reconciliation.

Oh, to sing a song before the dying has begun.
Oh, to look at the morning sky and see the sun.

An ocean of purple clouds to disappear in.
A love as real as blood.

It's been a week and still I am outside myself.
I reach the intersection of need and belief.

YOU AND ME

It occurred to me one golden morning that
music can wound, can be so right
it hurts.

Later, I raised my eyes and there was turbulence—
great, white palaces of clouds massing on the horizon—
between the coming and going, the infinity of sky.

These are the roads of song, the gradual slope
of day's light.

I have questions without answers:

If everything dances, what remains of solidity?
If the foundation is rotten, how long will the house last?
Are there truly roads in the air?

There is a song with no one to sing it.

It moves in silence, like the night—
It comes on a bleeding wing and is not mistaken.

There is matter where it doesn't matter,
There are empty holes that make us whole.

LOVE POEM

your lilting laugh warms me, sibilant words trickle off your tongue,
tiny pellets of air against the smooth whiteness of your neck,

the plunge of cleavage above the neckline of your black dress.
I shudder with desire, want to hold you in my arms press your body
to mine.

The mist has parted, the haze has fled on steel wheels, the fog has cleared,
yet there are places I am not allowed to go; crackling behind the curtain

is every day of which I am uncertain. I sit and wince and wonder
at the wonder
that is you. mysteries come and depart, tear at the wind. though at times

our stars align, the chaos that is my life may consume all the good
between us.
eyes grow dim, two faded orbs of pale blue; that woman you will become,
is you,

your painted face, your flowing hair. gazing at you my sight is clear.
in years to come it will fade and flee like a flock of geese careering
northward

against the deepening blue of a Midwestern sky. I follow the signs that lead
me to your heart, mine aligned with yours, my lust overshadowed by my
love for you.

I have not found you wanting.
I have found you waiting.

DARK WATERS

My love speaks of dark waters, of oceans of gray clouds.
We breathe the last breaths of evening; a shadow looms

above us as we sit at the foot of an oak tree dreaming
our lives away. A maiden dances among the falling
leaves; her song is silence, floating upwards on a spiraling

staircase of air. Small steps have led my love and me first away
from our goals and then with a billowy rush back—
our future, roaring towards us upon a cresting wave.

As the evening wanes there is an interlude, a time for relaxing
and chatting with one another, music through ear buds,
together we review the weekend past.

It is here that we want to be, calm and quiet
after the noises of the day, the conversations

we have with ourselves.

When my child's laughter comes from across a room
I realize my dreams have all come true.

ACKNOWLEDGMENTS

Grateful acknowledgment is made to the editors of the following journals where these poems, sometimes in earlier versions and under different titles, first appeared:

34th Parallel Magazine: "Hurt"

Sincerely Magazine: "Descent"

Soundings East: "Night Sky With Implications"

Torrid Literature Journal: "Body Check"

Check out more from Errol Rubenstein at
errol-rubenstein.com